What Makes Me A
PROTESTANT?

Adam Woog

KIDHAVEN PRESS
An imprint of Thomson Gale, a part of The Thomson Corporation

THOMSON
★
GALE

Detroit • New York • San Francisco • San Diego • New Haven, Conn.
Waterville, Maine • London • Munich

For Karen, the Protestant half of our union.

© 2005 Thomson Gale, a part of The Thomson Corporation.

Thomson and Star Logo are trademarks and Gale and KidHaven Press are registered trademarks used herein under license.

For more information, contact
KidHaven Press
27500 Drake Rd.
Farmington Hills, MI 48331-3535
Or you can visit our Internet site at http://www.gale.com

LIBRARY OF CONGRESS CATALOGING-IN-PUBLICATION DATA

Woog, Adam, 1953–
    Protestant / by Adam Woog
        p. cm. — (What Makes Me a?)
Summary: Discusses Protestantism including how the religion began, what Protestants believe, how they practice their faith, and what holidays they celebrate.
Includes bibliographical references and index.
ISBN 0-7377-2264-9 (hardcover : alk. paper)
1. Protestantism. 2. Protestant churches. I. Title. II. Series.
bx4811.3.W66 2004
280'4—dc22

2004009043

Printed in the United States of America

CONTENTS

CHAPTER ONE

How Did Protestantism Begin?

Protestants belong to many religious groups. The groups differ from each other in many ways, but Protestants are united in one important way. They are all Christians.

Christianity is based on the life and teachings of Jesus Christ, who lived about two thousand years ago. Jesus taught a message of love, peace, and simplicity. Christians believe that Jesus Christ is the Son of God, who was sent to earth to forgive humans for their sins and so allow them to enter heaven.

Christianity, which includes Protestantism, Catholicism, and the Eastern Orthodox Church, is the world's largest and most widespread religion. About 360 million people are Protestants, making it second in size to Catholicism among the Christian religions.

Protestantism was born in Europe in the 1500s. At that time, only one Christian church existed. (Today, it is known as the Catholic Church.) The church was widespread and powerful. However, a number of people were dissatisfied with some church leaders and their practices.

What They Objected To

The protesters objected to many aspects of the Catholic Church. One was the use of Latin as the only language for church services. Few ordinary people understood Latin, and many wanted to worship in their own languages.

The protesters also were angry about widespread corruption (illegal practices) within the church. For example, they accused some church leaders of collecting money

Jesus speaks with his followers in this painting. Like all Christians, Protestants believe Jesus is the Son of God.

In this sixteenth-century woodcut, the Pope pardons the sins of Christians who donate money to the church.

for the church but spending it on their own lavish lifestyles.

Also, the church's beliefs and worship services had become too complex for many protesters. They wanted to return to the simpler spiritual style of early Christianity. The protesters also rejected Catholicism's human religious authority, a person (called the pope) who dictated beliefs to the church's members.

Furthermore, the protesters objected to the use of all of the **sacraments**, sacred rituals that were (and still are) important parts of Catholic worship. There are seven holy sacraments in the Catholic faith, but generally the protesters accepted only the two that are specifically mentioned in the Bible, Christianity's most sacred book.

The Reformation

For decades, various religious leaders tried to break away from the church. However, the church was so powerful that it was able to control the protesters and keep them from forming new churches. They did this by accusing such rebels of **heresy.** Heresy meant that these people were committing crimes against the church and could be severely punished or even killed.

The church's power held until the early 1500s, when a number of groups finally amassed enough power of their own to begin breaking away. These protesters were called Protestants. Because they were asking for religious reforms, their movement became known as the **Reformation**.

One of the Reformation's leaders was a German **monk** named Martin Luther. Luther is well known for performing one act that was critical of the powerful church. Many people feel that this event marked the true beginning of Protestantism.

The Ninety-Five Theses

Luther's act was to write a list of ninety-five criticisms called theses. (A thesis is an argument or statement.) According to legend, he then nailed this list to the door of a church in Germany in 1517. Typical of the

Ninety-five Theses was an objection to the church's practice of selling **indulgences**. Indulgences allowed people to be forgiven of their **sins** if they donated money to the church. Luther strongly condemned the practice.

His arguments were widely circulated in Europe and caused a great deal of controversy. The church authorities punished Luther severely for making his criticisms public. They **excommunicated** him from the church. They also declared him a criminal, so that his life was in danger. Luther was forced to go into hiding and disguise himself.

However, he continued to speak out. He also formed his own church, which in time became the Lutheran Church. It differed from the Catholic Church in many ways. For example, it rejected the pope and claimed that God and his holy word, the Bible, were the only true religious authorities.

Loosely Linked but Separate

Luther's example inspired many other religious leaders across Europe. A number of Protestant **denominations** (religious groups) formed. Among these were the Puritan, Baptist, Reformed, and Anglican (Episcopalian). Still other denominations, including the Quaker, Presbyterian, and Methodist, formed later. Each group had its own separate practices and beliefs, so that a single, united Protestant Church never formed. Nonetheless, the groups were loosely linked by the same basic ideas.

These new religious movements attracted many people. By the mid-1500s, Protestantism of one sort or

The Protestant Reformation began in 1517 when Martin Luther (pictured) publicly criticized the Catholic Church and formed his own church.

another was dominant in about half of Europe. It became so widespread in some countries, especially in northern Europe, that it was the official national religion.

The Catholic Church tried hard to fight the Reformation. Violent conflicts between Catholics and Protestants

The Cradle of Protestantism

A crowd gathers to read Luther's theses in Wittenberg on October 31, 1517.

North
Sea

London O

Berlin O

Marburg
Wittenberg

Worms
Leipzig

Paris O

Augsburg

Mediterranean Sea

Rome O

Europe's Religious Divisions in 1560

- Protestant (all denominations)
- Roman Catholic
- Shared Territories
- Extent of Revolt from Catholic Church

often resulted, such as the Thirty Years' War. This was a series of bitter, bloody, and destructive battles between the Holy Roman Empire (a group of nations linked by Catholicism) and various Protestant countries and royalty.

In time, however, most of the fighting died down. When it did, Europe remained divided in its religious beliefs. Generally, Protestantism was strongest in northern European countries like Sweden, England, Germany, and Denmark.

Spreading to the New World

During and after the Reformation, Protestants were often **persecuted** (treated badly) because of their beliefs. They were not always able to live freely or worship as they

In the 1600s many Protestants came to North America. Here, Protestants give thanks before eating with a group of Native Americans.

chose. Sometimes they were tortured or killed because of their beliefs. As a result, many traveled to North America when Europeans began settling it in the 1600s.

Life was uncertain, rough, and often dangerous there. However, it was worth it for the promise of religious freedom. As a result, many Protestant groups, such as the Quakers and the Puritans, found homes in North America.

Protestantism grew steadily there during the next centuries. By the mid-1800s, it was the largest faith in English-speaking North America (and still is). It was also divided into many more different groups.

CHAPTER TWO

What Forms Does Protestantism Take?

Although Protestantism began with just a handful of denominations, today hundreds, perhaps thousands, exist. One estimate puts the number at thirty thousand.

Many Groups

Some of the best-known Protestant groups today are the Baptist, Episcopalian (Anglican), and Lutheran churches. Also prominent are the Methodist, Presbyterian, United Church of Christ, and Unitarian denominations. Still others are the African Methodist Episcopal, Amish, Brethren, Christian Science, Jehovah's Witnesses, Mennonite (Anabaptist), Pentecostal, Quaker (Friends), Salvation Army, and Seventh-Day Adventist churches.

Some of these groups, such as the Baptists, Lutherans, and Methodists, are very large. They have been in existence for hundreds of years. Each has millions of members, from all walks of life, all around the world.

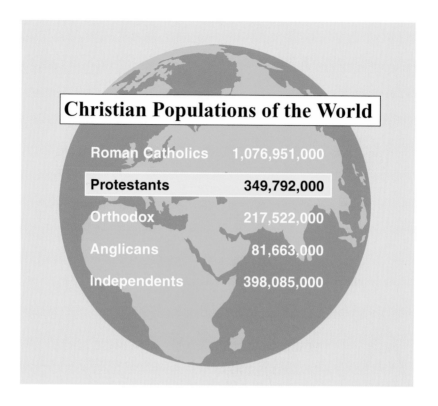

Christian Populations of the World

Roman Catholics	1,076,951,000
Protestants	349,792,000
Orthodox	217,522,000
Anglicans	81,663,000
Independents	398,085,000

Others, such as the Pentecostals, have formed more recently, quickly becoming large and fast-growing organizations that span the world. And there are many other, smaller Protestant churches. The tiniest of them might have only a handful of members who worship in a single building.

Reaching Out

Each Protestant denomination has characteristics that set it apart from the others. For example, some branches believe especially strongly in the importance of service—that is, helping others. Inspired by Jesus's message of compassion, they place great importance on improving the lives of the poor or disadvantaged.

Lutherans are just one of the many Protestant groups that have well-established services to help people who belong to their church as well as others. These services typically include such agencies as adoption organizations, health clinics, and senior centers. Church service organizations also sponsor international aid efforts to help the victims of war, disaster, or famine. Another familiar example of service to others is that of the Salvation Army, whose bell-ringing workers collect money for the needy on street corners.

Another way churches reach out to help others is to work on broad campaigns to improve society. One

A Salvation Army worker collects money on a street corner. Protestant groups like the Salvation Army help people in need.

example is that of overseas human rights watches. Many religious groups such as the Quakers sponsor projects that try to ensure that human rights are honored in countries that have histories of abuse.

Sometimes Protestant groups reach out in still other ways. For example, some focus on the importance of **evangelizing**—that is, gaining **converts** (new members). The Seventh-Day Adventist church is among those that are especially active in evangelizing. They do this through such efforts as overseas missionary work or talking to people door-to-door.

Rejecting Some Modern Lifestyles

Some denominations reject modern lifestyles. These groups choose to lead nonstandard lives because of certain ways they interpret Christian beliefs. A well-known example is the Amish community.

The Amish originated hundreds of years ago in Europe, but they now live primarily in Pennsylvania and other parts of America. They reject much of mainstream society, in part because they believe that modern technology tends to distract people from the simple life that Jesus taught.

Because of the lives they lead, the Amish are known as the Plain People. They dress simply and live in tightly knit farming communities, worshipping in their homes instead of in churches and often speaking German among themselves. The Amish also reject modern inventions such as electricity or cars. Instead, they use lanterns or candles for light, nonelectric forms of power

Amish farmers in Pennsylvania use a horse-drawn plow in their fields. The Amish reject all modern inventions.

such as windmills, and horse-drawn buggies for transportation. Furthermore, like the Quakers and the Brethren, they believe in nonviolence.

Other Nonstandard Religious Lives

Another denomination that turns away from an aspect of modern society is the Church of Christ, Scientist (Christian Science). Christian Scientists reject the use of doctors and medicine. Instead, they trust in the power of prayer to heal their illnesses, believing that their mental and physical health is completely in God's hands.

Jehovah's Witnesses refuse to have blood transfusions (that is, donating blood or receiving it from others). They believe that this practice goes against several biblical passages that forbid people from eating blood. Jehovah's Witnesses have interpreted these passages to include blood transfusions.

Some Protestants follow strict diets and do not eat meat or drink alcoholic or caffeinated beverages.

Still another example of a Protestant group turning away from an aspect of modern society is that of the Seventh-Day Adventists. Strict Adventists do not eat meat or drink liquor or caffeine. They believe that these and certain other foods and spices tend to stimulate people in an unhealthy way.

Strict and Less Strict

Some denominations are not especially set apart from other groups by the ways in which they live their lives. Rather, their views on religion sharply differ from other Protestants. One example is a group of denominations that together are called the Pentecostal (Charismatic) churches. These churches are among those that support a religious view called Fundamentalism.

According to Fundamentalism, the Bible is the literal word of God. Therefore, every word of the Bible must be completely true. Because of this interpretation, Fundamentalists reject such ideas as the theory of evolution. They choose instead to believe the Bible's statement that God created the entire world and everything on it within just a few days.

Just as they are very strict in their views about the Bible, Fundamentalists are generally also strict in the way they regard society, family, and moral standards. For example, many forbid their members to smoke or drink alcohol. Some churches forbid their members to dance or attend movies and plays.

On the other hand, some Protestant denominations are far less strict. For example, Unitarians and some

Protestants pray in a Pentecostal church in Guatemala. Pentecostal Protestants believe the Bible is the literal word of God.

Quakers do not believe that the Bible is literally true. They instead consider it to be a book of very important lessons that reveal simple but deep spiritual truths.

The groups mentioned here are just a few of the many denominations that have formed within Protestantism. Each is different in its own way. Despite their differences and variations, however, the various Protestant denominations all share certain basic beliefs and traditions.

CHAPTER THREE

What Do Protestants Believe?

Perhaps the most important of the basic beliefs shared by all Christians is the belief in only one God. Protestants believe that this single God created and controls everything in the universe. He is all-powerful.

Furthermore, Protestants generally believe that God is good, loving, and forgiving of human sins. (A sin is a bad word or deed that goes against God or against people.) According to Protestant teachings, He should be worshipped and honored above all else. And it is possible for all people to have a personal relationship with Him.

The majority of Protestants believe that God takes three forms. This trio is called the Holy Trinity. (*Trinity* means three.) The three forms are God in heaven, Jesus, and the Holy Spirit. The Holy Spirit is God's presence in the world. It comforts people in times of trouble and helps them always to keep God in their hearts.

(The major exception to this general belief is in Unitarian thought. The Unitarians question the idea of the Holy Trinity.)

The messages of love, compassion, worship, and simplicity that Jesus taught are also central to virtually all forms of Protestantism. According to Protestant teachings, Jesus was the Messiah, the Son of God. He was sent to earth as the savior of humanity, died so that humanity's sins could be forgiven, and was resurrected to rejoin God in heaven. According to general Protestant belief, Jesus will return again someday to lead the world in a period of peace and harmony.

The Bible

Belief in the importance of the Bible is another basic cornerstone of Protestantism. The Bible is in two parts: the Old and New testaments. The Old Testament is ancient, and it tells stories about God and the early days of the world. It also predicts that the Messiah will come someday. The New Testament, among other things, relates the life and teachings of Jesus. It was written in the years after Jesus's death.

To different degrees, however, various branches of Protestantism have different beliefs about the Bible's importance as a source of religious knowledge. To some denominations, such as the Lutherans, no other written or human source but the Bible is necessary to find and maintain a relationship with God. This is in keeping with Martin Luther's belief that the Bible is the supreme source of religious knowledge.

Most Protestants believe in the Holy Trinity of God, Jesus, and the Holy Spirit (shown in this painting as a dove).

Other denominations, such as the Unitarians, often feel differently. These groups may regard the Bible as a sacred and holy text. However, they also find inspiration in other sources and do not believe the Bible is the only source of religious knowledge.

Other Sources

In some cases, these other texts were written by early Christians, such as Saint Paul. Paul was an early convert to

Christianity and one of its greatest writers and thinkers. His quest for a deeper understanding of God still inspires many Protestants today on their own spiritual journeys.

Some denominations use more recently written sources in addition to the Bible or the writings of the early Christians. For example, Episcopalians use the *Book of Common Prayer,* which dates from the mid-1500s. Christian Scientists use *Science and Health with Key to the Scriptures,* which was first published in 1875.

In still other cases, Protestants are open to insights from many other sources—even non-Christian sources. For example, some Unitarians and some Quakers are open to studying Buddhism or other Eastern religions.

Saint Paul preaches to a crowd in Greece. The writings of Paul are very important to many Protestants.

They feel that religious insight and inspiration can and should come from many diverse sources.

The Importance of Faith

Another belief common to Protestantism as a whole concerns the importance of **salvation**. Salvation means being saved. To be saved means to achieve a state of grace—that is, to be in God's good favor.

According to most Protestants, a person who is in a state of grace will be guaranteed a place in heaven after death. In heaven, people will enjoy the peaceful and serene presence of God for all time. Some Protestants believe that anyone who is not saved will spend an eternity of torment in hell. That is, they will be forever denied the peace of God's presence.

Connected to salvation is the idea of sin. If a person is saved, then he or she has been cleansed of all sins. Generally speaking, most Protestant denominations believe that all people are born sinners, and that they will continue to sin throughout their lives. They cannot do otherwise. Because they are unable to be free of sin on their own, they will not be able to achieve salvation by themselves.

However, according to Protestant faith, a belief in God and Jesus can help them achieve salvation. If people have faith in God, then God will accept them. He will forgive everyone, including sinners, and grant them grace. This gift from God is freely given. It is called **justification**.

The belief in one God, the importance of Jesus's lessons of simplicity and love, reverence for the Bible, the

A Methodist woman prays to God to forgive her sins. Protestants believe only God can save people from sin.

idea of achieving salvation through justification—these are some of the basic beliefs from which Protestantism was born. But in Protestantism, as in other religions, the ways in which people practice their faith—using their beliefs in daily life—can be as important as faith itself.

These ways of putting faith into action take many different forms, just as Protestant beliefs take many different forms. However, Protestants do generally share some practices in common.

CHAPTER FOUR

How Do Protestants Practice Their Faith?

The primary way in which Protestants practice their faith is through worship. Leading the way in this are formal religious leaders called **ministers**. (Some denominations call them pastors, while Episcopalians call them priests.)

Within Protestantism, the role of minister varies widely. For example, Jehovah's Witnesses consider everyone to be a minister with a duty to spread God's word. On the other hand, some Quaker groups do not have pastors at all. They believe that all people are equal, and that ministers are not needed because everyone has a direct connection to God.

The Role of Ministers

In a typical denomination, a minister or pastor plays an important role in the lives of the **congregation** (group of regular church members). Typically, ministers run the church, organize the regular services, and perform important ceremonies such as marriages and sacraments. They supervise activities such as fund-raising efforts or youth groups. Ministers also help out individual church members who are ill, in need of counseling, or are otherwise unfortunate.

People who belong to a given congregation, but who are not ministers, are called **lay members** or the **laity**. These terms come from a Greek word meaning "the people." Lay members play important roles in Protestant churches. For example, they might help govern their churches' rules, organize fund-raising, maintain church buildings, and collect donations. Sometimes, lay members assist the minister during regular worship services.

Typically, Protestant ministers can marry and have families (unlike Catholic priests). In certain Protestant denominations, both men and women can become ministers. Some denominations are also open to the inclusion of gay ministers. However, others are fiercely opposed to this.

Baptism

Leading worship services is one of the most important jobs of a minister. Typically, the first experience that a Protestant has of these services is baptism. Baptism is one of the two sacraments that Protestants typically perform. It has been part of Christianity since the very earliest days. John the Baptist, an early Christian, performed it on Jesus.

Baptism represents the beginning of Christian life for new members. The minister uses water to wash away the person's sins ritually. This cleansing also symbolizes

Some Protestant denominations allow women to become ministers. Here, a Presbyterian minister talks with a member of her church.

the person's entry into the church. In some congregations, only a few drops are sprinkled. In others, water is poured on the person's head. And in some denominations, the person is completely submerged.

Many denominations, including Lutherans and Episcopalians, baptize infants. However, other groups, such as the Baptists, baptize only older children and adults. This is because they feel that the ceremony should symbolize faith that already exists. Therefore, a person must be old enough to make a mature decision about joining the church before baptism can occur. Some groups, including Christian Scientists and Quakers, do not perform baptism at all.

Worship Services

Baptism of infants or new members is typically part of a church worship service. Taking part in services on a regular basis helps Protestants in many ways. They can feel closer to God and Jesus. They are comforted in times of uncertainty or trouble. And they can stay closely involved in church and community life.

Protestants typically attend church on Sunday, the traditional Christian day of rest and prayer. However, some groups, such as Seventh-Day Adventists and Jehovah's Witnesses, hold services on Saturdays.

Worship services vary quite a bit, depending on the denomination. However, they do share some general characteristics. For instance, a typical service includes a **sermon** (religious speech) by the minister. These speeches are based on religion, but they can present opinion and guidance on many topics. For example, a sermon might reflect on an upcoming holiday or address a problem, such as crime, affecting the whole community.

The parts of a worship service usually follow a fixed order. In addition to a sermon, for instance, a worship service usually includes welcoming statements, **hymns** (sacred songs), prayers, musical interludes, and Bible readings. Bible readings are often tied to the time of year and the observances of the religious calendar.

Communion

Central to most Protestant worship services is the performance of communion (sometimes called the Lord's Supper). This sacred ritual is the other sacrament besides baptism that Protestants typically perform. It also has been performed continuously for thousands of years.

Communion recalls and honors Jesus's words and actions at his last meal. Jesus blessed some bread and wine and said to his followers, "This is my body. This is my blood. Do this in memory of me."

During the ceremony today, people swallow a bit of bread and drink a sip of wine or juice. The bread and liquid have been blessed by the minister. These things, representing Jesus's blood and body, symbolize God's forgiveness of sinners. In some denominations, everyone

During a Sunday service, a Protestant minister shares a sermon with her congregation that offers them spiritual help.

drinks from one cup and tears a piece of bread from one loaf. Others use special wafers and individual cups.

Some Protestant churches perform communion once a week. Others do it only once or twice a month, or even once every three months. Of the main denominations, the Episcopalians and Lutherans are strictest about observing it often.

In order to take communion, the members of many denominations must first go through a ceremony called confirmation. This usually is for young adults of twelve to fourteen, and it marks entry into the church as a full member. It is called confirmation because it confirms (strengthens) the ritual of baptism.

Episcopalians kneel as they take communion from their minister. Communion is the most important part of Protestant worship services.

Quiet or Noisy

As is true for all Christian denominations, prayer is a vital part of Protestant services. Sometimes prayers are spoken out loud by the entire congregation. However, silent and private prayer is also important. This meditation reflects the belief that all Protestants maintain personal relationships with God.

Some services are especially quiet. For example, Quaker meetings for worship, as they are called, have long periods of silence. During these silences, people speak out, reflecting on God or other topics, only when they feel moved to do so.

In contrast to this, some services seem almost rowdy. For example, in many Baptist and Pentecostal churches the ministers and congregation grow passionate in their celebrations. Sermons are shouted out and the choir sings joyously. In some Pentecostal denominations, people might speak in tongues—that is, they say things in unknown languages. Such behavior reflects the belief that God's Holy Spirit can actively possess people.

Typically, a Protestant worship service ends with a closing hymn and a benediction. This prayer expresses the hope that God's blessings will be with everyone.

Regular worship services are routine parts of Protestants' daily lives. But those lives also include special occasions called holidays.

CHAPTER FIVE

What Holidays Do Protestants Celebrate?

Holidays can be serious times for reflection and prayer. They can also be joyous celebrations where family, friends, and community members gather together. Many holidays combine both the serious and the joyous.

There is a great deal of variety concerning Protestant holidays, however. Many holidays are shared by most Protestants. Some are celebrated by some denominations, but not by others. Some holidays, meanwhile, are unique to certain denominations.

Meanwhile, some Protestants do not observe holidays at all. For instance, some Quaker groups believe that no day is more sacred than any other, so they do not generally observe holidays. Nor do Jehovah's Witnesses observe holidays. In their teachings, holidays like Christmas and Easter are ancient **pagan** festivals. (*Pagan* refers to religions that are not Christian, Jewish, or Muslim.) Also, the Jehovah's Witnesses strive to model themselves on early Christians, who did not celebrate Christmas or Easter.

Christmas

Despite these exceptions, most Protestants do celebrate the major Christian holidays. One of these falls on December 25—Christmas Day, which celebrates the birth of Jesus. (The exact day of his birth has never been pinpointed. However, it has been celebrated on December 25 since A.D. 350.)

A Methodist girl lights a candle during a Christmas Eve service. Protestants celebrate the birth of Jesus with special Christmas services.

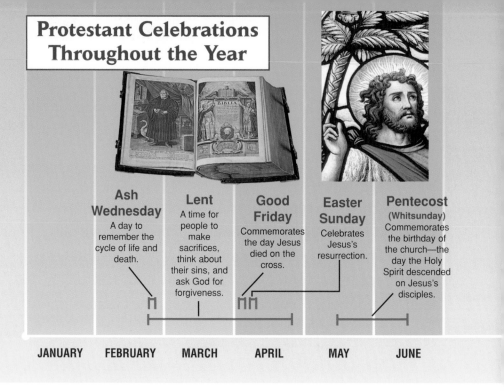

Protestant Celebrations Throughout the Year

Ash Wednesday	Lent	Good Friday	Easter Sunday	Pentecost
A day to remember the cycle of life and death.	A time for people to make sacrifices, think about their sins, and ask God for forgiveness.	Commemorates the day Jesus died on the cross.	Celebrates Jesus's resurrection.	(Whitsunday) Commemorates the birthday of the church—the day the Holy Spirit descended on Jesus's disciples.

JANUARY FEBRUARY MARCH APRIL MAY JUNE

The weeks leading up to Christmas form a period called Advent. In some ways, the Advent season is a time for serious reflection. People try especially hard to think about and follow Jesus's example of generosity and tolerance.

But Advent is also a joyous time. Family members gather together and people usually get time off from work or school. Traditionally, people also decorate their houses and give presents to each other.

On Christmas Eve, December 24, and on Christmas Day, Protestant churches hold special services. Ministers deliver special sermons at these times. They talk about what they feel the occasion of Jesus's birth can mean in today's world.

The Easter Season

Just as Christmas celebrates Jesus's birth, Easter commemorates Jesus's death, resurrection, and ascent into

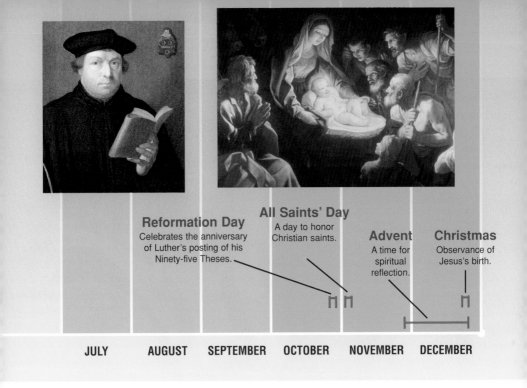

Reformation Day
Celebrates the anniversary
of Luther's posting of his
Ninety-five Theses.

All Saints' Day
A day to honor
Christian saints.

Advent
A time for
spiritual
reflection.

Christmas
Observance of
Jesus's birth.

JULY   AUGUST   SEPTEMBER   OCTOBER   NOVEMBER   DECEMBER

heaven. It is a month-long celebration, with special services and rituals along the way. Easter arrives in the spring, in late March or early April, but the exact date differs every year. This is because it is determined by the movement of the moon.

Many Protestant denominations, such as the Episcopalians, Methodists, and Lutherans, have special observations during Holy Week, the week leading up to Easter. Among these is Ash Wednesday, when priests mark a cross of ashes on people's foreheads.

In ancient times, such a mark indicated ownership of slaves, so the cross symbolizes that the person belongs to Jesus. Also, it reminds people of the Bible passage that states, "from dust thou art [you are], and unto dust shalt thou [you shall] return." This passage means that all people come from the earth and will someday return to it.

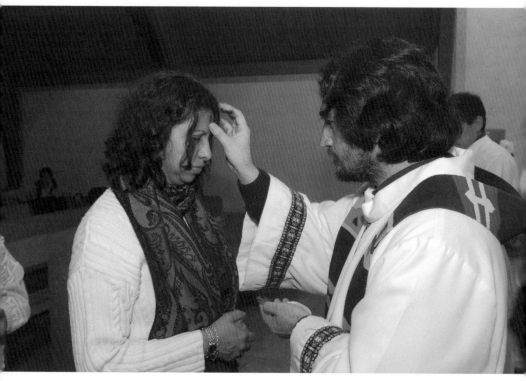

Some Protestants celebrate Ash Wednesday, when priests mark a cross of ashes on people's foreheads.

Other Easter Observances

Other special days during Holy Week include Palm Sunday and Good Friday. On Palm Sunday, people go to church for a ceremony in which they receive crosses made of palm leaves. This recalls the time Jesus rode into Jerusalem, when people waved palm leaves as a sign of welcome. Good Friday services, meanwhile, are solemn occasions to honor the day when Jesus died.

Throughout Holy Week, many Protestant churches hold services meant for any and all denominations of Christianity, not just their specific group. These services, called interdenominational services, are designed to focus attention on the things that all Christians share. They emphasize the beliefs that unify the various denominations, rather than the things that separate them.

Holy Week activities lead up to Easter Sunday. On this, the single most important day in the Protestant religious calendar, churches often hold sunrise services. These symbolize the light that returned to the world with Jesus's resurrection. They also symbolize the belief that, with faith, everyone can be reborn as Jesus was.

Throughout the rest of the year, most Protestants also celebrate other holidays, such as Pentecost. Pentecost, also called Whitsunday, falls on the fiftieth day

Worshippers attend a sunrise service on Easter Sunday, the most important day in the Protestant religious calendar.

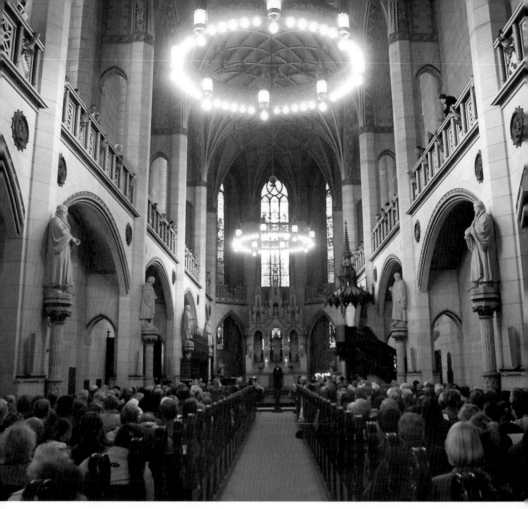

Lutherans celebrate Reformation Day in the church in Wittenberg, Germany, where Martin Luther posted his Ninety-five Theses.

after Easter. It commemorates the Holy Spirit descending on Jesus's early disciples.

Other Holidays

One holiday that is unique to Protestantism is Reformation Day, celebrated on October 31 (or sometimes on the last Sunday in October). Reformation Day celebrates the anniversary of Luther's legendary posting of his Ninety-five Theses on October 31, 1517.

In some European countries where Protestantism dominates, Reformation Day is an important holiday, when schools and government buildings are closed and many people have a day off work. In America, it is less important, but many churches still hold special services that focus on the Reformation and its impact on the world. Some churches also sponsor Reformation Day parties for kids, with games and plays that commemorate the origins of their religion.

Celebrating holidays is just one of the ways in which Protestants act on their religious beliefs. Worshipping, in private or in church, is another way. And a third is to put faith into action through service—that is, by helping other people who may be less fortunate. All of these are ways in which Protestants honor their long-held traditions and strengthen their deep faith in God.

GLOSSARY

congregation: The people who attend an individual church.

converts: New members to a religious group.

denomination: A specific religious group or religion.

evangelizing: Spreading religious education by telling other people.

excommunication: The act of expelling someone from the Catholic Church.

heresy: Saying something that goes against standard teachings or beliefs.

hymns: Sacred songs.

indulgences: Acts that allowed people to be forgiven sins if they donated money to the Catholic Church.

justification: The idea that God grants forgiveness to sinners.

laity or **lay members:** Those members of a congregation who are not formal religious leaders.

ministers: Protestant religious leaders. Some denominations call their leaders pastors.

monks: Members of the Catholic Church structure who devote themselves full-time to lives of religious study, prayer, and service.

pagan: A religion that is not Christian, Jewish, or Muslim.

persecuted: To be treated badly because of religious beliefs.

Reformation: The name given to the events when Protestants broke away from the Catholic Church.

sacraments: Sacred rituals that were (and still are) important parts of Catholic worship. Some sacraments are also part of most Protestant worship services.

salvation: The idea of being saved and spending eternity with God.

sermon: A lecture during a church service on some religious subject.

sin: A bad word or deed against God or other people.

FOR FURTHER EXPLORATION

Books

John Logan, *Christianity*. New York: Thomson Learning, 1995. This book, part of a series on world religions, is a good introduction to all of Christianity, including Protestantism.

Philemon D. Sevastiades, *I Am Protestant*. New York: Rosen Group, 1996. A simple introduction in the Religions of the World series.

Lawrence E. Sullivan, *The Theses of Protestantism*. Philadelphia: Chelsea House, 2002. Written for older readers, but with many good illustrations.

Web Sites

ChristianityToday.com (www.ctlibrary.com/3874). Not designed for children, but with some good quotes from Protestantism's founder.

Clubhouse (www.clubhousemagazine.com). On this site maintained by the Christian organization Focus on the Family, kids can find games, Bible stories, true stories about Christian experiences, and more.

Holidays on the Net (www.holidays.net). This site for kids explores holidays from many faiths.

INDEX

INDEX

Jesus Christ
    Christmas and, 35–36
    Easter and, 36–39
    message of, 4
    as Messiah, 22
John the Baptist, 28
justification, 25

Latin, 5
lay members/laity, 28
leaders, 28
    see also ministers
Luther, Martin, 7–8, 40
Lutherans
    baptism and, 29
    beginning of, 8
    Bible and, 22
    characteristics of, 15
    communion and, 32
    Holy Week and, 37–39
    number of, 13–14

marriage, 28
medical care, 17–18
Methodists
    Holy Week and, 37–39
    number of, 13–14
ministers
    duties of, 27–28
    worship services and, 28–32
missionary work, 16

New Testament, 22
Ninety-five Theses, 7–8, 40
North America, 11–12

Old Testament, 22

Palm Sunday, 38
pastors. *See* ministers
Pentecost, 39–40
Pentecostals (Charismatics)
    Fundamentalism and, 19
    growth of, 14
    worship services of, 33
Plain People, 16–17

prayers, 33
Protestantism
    beginning of, 4–8
    number of believers of, 4
    spread of, 8–9, 11–12

Quakers
    baptism and, 29
    Bible and, 20
    Eastern religions and, 24–25
    holidays and, 34
    human rights and, 16
    pastors and, 27
    worship services of, 33

Reformation, 7–8, 9, 11
Reformation Day, 40–41

sacraments, 6–7, 28
Saint Paul, 23–24
salvation, 25
Salvation Army, 15
sermons, 30
service groups, 15–16
Seventh-Day Adventists
    diet of, 19
    missionary work and, 16
    worship services of, 30
sin, 25, 31
speaking in tongues, 33
state of grace, 25

Thirty Years' War, 11

Unitarians
    Bible and, 19–20, 23
    Eastern religions and, 24–25

Whitsunday, 39–40
worship services
    baptism and, 28–29
    communion and, 30–32
    interdenominational, 39
    noise during, 33
    parts of, 30, 33
    see also holidays

PICTURE CREDITS

ABOUT THE AUTHOR

Adam Woog is the author of many books for adults, young adults, and children. He grew up in Seattle, Washington, and lives there with his wife and daughter.